Calling

*. . . those maddening little women who kept calling,
calling to each other . . .*

"Brazil, January 1, 1502," Elizabeth Bishop

❧

Also by the same author

The Rhubarb King
Different Arrangements
But I Won't Go Out in a Boat
A Stranger in Her House
The Other Mozart

Calling

Poems by

Sharon Chmielarz

Loonfeather Press
Bemidji, Minnesota

Copyright © 2010 by Sharon Chmielarz
All rights reserved

Cover Art: *Our Olana* by Susan Gardner, used by permission. Olana means "our treasured house on high" in Latinized Arabic. It is the name of the painter Fredric Church's house on the Hudson and also Susan Gardner's daughter.

Cover Design: Mary Lou Marchand

First printing 2010
Printed in the United States
ISBN 978-0-926147-29-4

Loonfeather Press is a not-for-profit small press organized under section 501 (c) (3) of the United States Internal Revenue Code.

Loonfeather Press
P.O. Box 1212
Bemidji, MN 56619

Acknowledgments

Grateful acknowledgment is made to the following publications in which the following poems, sometimes in a slightly different form, first appeared:

"Burning," "Milton on the Plains," "The Coal Furnace" in *The Iowa Review;* "Subjects" in *Cutbank Review;* "A Christmas Story . . . of a Sort" in *Prairie Schooner;* "Jephthah's Daughter" as "Jephthah and His Daughter" in *Notre Dame Review;* "Monet's Egg Girl" and "The Burgermeister's Wife's Account" as "She Was" in *Margie, The American Journal of Poetry;* "Mrs. Heinike and Mr. Mendelssohn" in *The Mid American Poetry Review;* "Dog Days in Court, 1780s" published as "A Brief History of Wilhelmina, Margravine of Bayreuth" in *The American Voice;* "Roseteeth" in *The Seneca Review;* "Red, Red Rose; a Loose, Loose Story" in *The Laurel Review;* "In Each Other's Hair" in *The Chiron Review;* "On the Death of His Sister: Goethe's Winter Journey," "Wax Cylinder Recordings: Riffs from a Small Town," "On the Train to Milan" in *Water-Stone;* "McIntosh, South Dakota" in *The North Dakota Review;* "Now It's Late" in *Briar Cliff Review;* "Akhmatova's Place" in *Speakeasy;* "Pictures from an Extinction: The Motherland" in *Southern Poetry Review;* "Three Faces" in *North American Review;* "The Beekeepers" in *Ekphrasis;* "On Brothers: A Conversation Between Dorothy Wordsworth and Nannerl Mozart" in *Phoebe, SUNY-Oneonta;* "View from Porch" in *Turtle Quarterly.*

"The Beekeepers" received a Pushcart nomination.

My thanks to the many wonderful poets and editors who've read and suggested revisions to this work over the years. Special thanks go to Betty Rossi, Gail Rixen and Mary Lou Marchand at Loonfeather Press.

for my sisters

CONTENTS

I. The Culture Club

Subjects (four parts) ~ 3
Roseteeth ~ 5
The Beekeepers (six parts) ~ 6
Mrs. Heinicke and Mr. Mendelssohn ~ 8
Dog Days in Court, 1780s ~ 9
   Then Berlin ~ 9
   My Arrival in Bayreuth ~ 9
   The New Margravine's Reign ~ 10
   Betrayal ~ 11
   Aftermath, Enduring Love ~ 11
On Brothers: A Conversation Between Dorothy Wordsworth and Nannerl Mozart ~ 12
Music, I Must Have Music ~ 14
On the Death of His Sister: Goethe's Winter Journey ~ 15
"Dear Little Sister"—Wil van Gogh ~ 17
Wonder Woman at Seventy ~ 18
The Bird Men ~ 19

II. Home

Wax Cylinder Recordings: Riffs from a Small Town ~ 25
   1. A Shirt to Wear ~ 25
   2. Did You Hear That? ~ 25
   3. Response to "Letters to the Editor" ~ 26
   4. The Sixth District Women's Convention ~ 27
   5. Drive ~ 27
   6. I Get Her Name Into Print ~ 28
   7. Other Women ~ 28

In Each Other's Hair ~ 30
Lucifer at the Supper Table ~ 31
Milton on the Plains: The Coal Furnace ~ 32
McIntosh, South Dakota ~33
Now It's Late ~ 34
Fruit Closet ~ 35

III. Behind the Curtain

Pictures from an Extinction: The Motherland ~ 39
Three Faces ~ 41
Akhmatova's Place ~ 42
Stalin's Daughter ~ 43
A Christmas Story . . . of a Sort ~ 44
The Burgermeister's Wife's Account ~ 45
The Last Queen of France ~ 46
Jephthah's Daughter ~ 47
Burning ~ 48

IV. And Then, Love

Monet's Egg Girl ~ 53
On the Train to Milan, the Conductor, *il Controllore* ~ 55
The Islanders ~ 57
View from Porch ~ 61
Mr. Schmier's Wife ~ 62
Red, Red Rose; a Loose, Loose Story ~ 63

V. Galileo's Daughter

Sister Marie Celeste (a poem in fourteen sayings)
  Money Solves Most Problems ~ 67
  The Heavenly Father Sends Our Earthly Father to Love Us ~ 67
  Earth Offers Us a Taste of Heaven ~ 68
  It Is No Wonder the Poor Are Poor in Spirit ~ 68

The Seasons Go Round in Order ~ 69
The Necessity for Wine Can't Be Ignored ~ 70
The Heart Is Often Embattled ~ 70
Good Wine: It Is But One Remedy for Good Health ~ 71
Lifting Up Your Heart Is Beneficial: Antiphon ~ 72
Love Is the Best War: Armor Yourself with Weapons ~ 72
One Sickens of Sickness ~ 73
A Small Garden Has the Large Garden's Troubles ~ 73
Luck Sometimes Occurs Naturally ~74
A Mystery Can Never Be Solved ~ 74

Notes ~76

I. The Culture Club

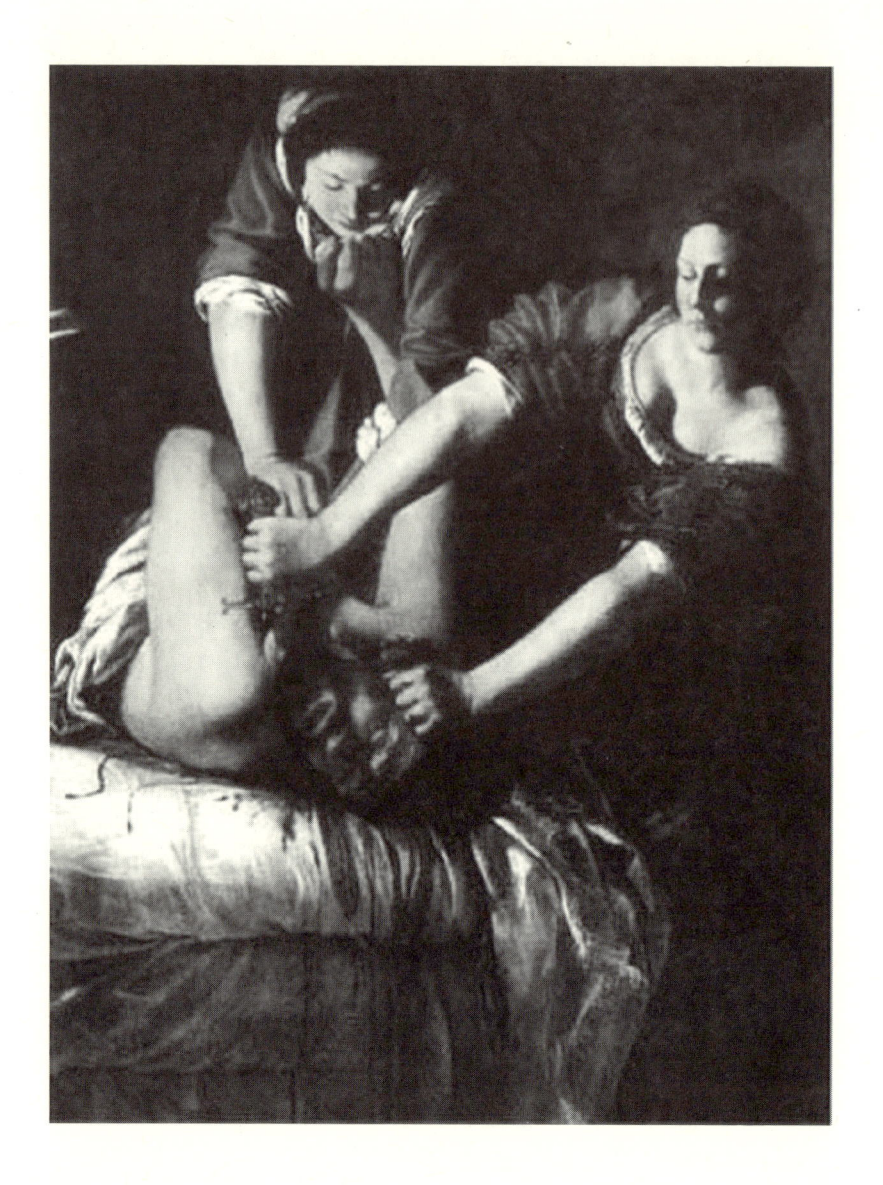

The copy of *Judith and Holofernes,* Artemesia Gentileschi, is used by kind permission of the photo archives in the Department of Historical Artistic and Ethnological Property and the Polo Museum of the City of Naples (Italy).

Subjects (four parts)
   —for Artemesia Gentileschi, 1593-1652

As to the paintings, hers were a Baroque
kind of home therapy, vicariously
sizing up her rapist as if he were
a plucked chicken, wielding her
brush like a knife, rendering him
the enemy in the Biblical story,
Judith Slaying Holofernes,
dispatch the job, written all over
the subject's, Judith's, face, mirroring
the painter's. The virgin-white sheet,
speckled with blood. The rapist's fist
balled against the female breast,
ever so weakly, due to a deep slit
in his jugular. And yet, vengeance
can be delicate. Look how tenderly,
in the painter's *Jael and Sisera*, Jael
pounds a peg into her enemy's ear. Sleep tight.

ꝏ

Maybe you call it lapis lazuli, maybe royal blue.
The fabric is rich as the first unfolded evening,
the premier gentian. Blue's throaty, trumpet voice.
Against a golden shift you have the stunning
first day and night in the firmament. You have
first cousin to the great. You have Judith,
in blue, her breasts slipping out of her bodice.

The heart beats wildly. Judith's maidservant
looks over her shoulder, fearing anyone
walking in on the act—catching the two women
carrying Holofernes' head off in a basket.
Such rustling satins, deep folds, dresses
as recitations of a story's favorite lines.
They do not want one single omission.

❧

A light meal with Giovanni Galileo and daughter.
Bread, cheese, olives on the table. The astronomer's
eyes, cloaked brilliance. He likes to hear the painter
talk about her work; he doesn't wish to see it.
She says she's sketching Susanna & the Elders,
but their heads are too cocked, they must seem
with her Susanna like the average authoritarians:
two men from the same small town,
whose blood pounds harder, taking a virgin.
Tomorrow, before someone calls her name, before
the baby wakes, before a creditor hounds the door,
before her body demands she leave the easel,
she'll get them right. In mock practice, over her plate,
the painter's hand poses like an asp before the strike.

❧

Cara, the painter's self-portrait. She reassures
her skin she loves it still. Even after the rapist
has handled it, her body is the ever-present
model for a rounded arm, a shadowed eye,
which side of the face to reveal.

Her hand flies, at work even in sleep,
when she reaches for her man, his sex, she
weighs its bulge, measuring what might be
Holofernes' size. Would robes diminish it?
So the only blob one sees is his severed head?

Her stove, her oven, the strip between
her legs, she is the hottest woman in Florence.
No one dare touch her. Before she even
enters a room, she's already painting
her reaction according to who sits where.

The beauty of an inner room! Jupiter's
sperm sprays as stars through the portico's
windows. A golden storm. It catches
her breath. She paints Danaï,
the subject, catching the stars in her fist.

4

Roseteeth

Not one rose at Versailles—
a court of uneven teeth,
yellowed, rotting structures—

not one rose ever
reneged on wearying
discipline, sitting

before a mirror, white rose
pallor like Madame Pompadour's
mouthful of perfect teeth.

The smile of a cut rose,
brocaded depths,
unacquainted with morning

ennui. Why have only
one or two of anything,
when more will do?

The Beekeepers (six parts)
  —pen and ink drawing by Pieter Bruegel the Elder, 1560s

Such beings! Hooded. In place of a face a basket
mask, a snoutless countenance, flat as an idiot's,
round protection woven from the medieval mind.
No iron visor necessary, no bee can penetrate
that hemp surface. But how can the keepers
breathe behind it? How can they see?
                                        It's sure
they've walked the path so often between meadow
and hillock, they can do it in their sleep, ditto tying,
sightless, their sock-like shoes and habit-robe,
a cross between a monk's (with slit in side) and stalking
ghost's. En route, they step around the magnificent
skunk cabbage Bruegel's drawn. The bees may be
the dashes swarming into millions of June leaves.

                ❧

Their voices, muzzled. Their thoughts
reduced to mime and habitual movement.
Their heads buzz from the breakfast beer,
or the beer drunk last night to cool them off
before they crawled, sweaty-haired and
sweaty-faced into bed, like bees crawling
into their hives, vincible, striking by instinct.

                ❧

What I'd thought was skunk cabbage is mandrake.
Mayapples is another name, a prettier reminder
of the scene from Eden. Beekeepers descend
from that nameless cousin who didn't eat of the apple.
God kept her in another part of the Garden.
She never questioned a bee's will.
Nor doubted a sting could hurt or kill.

❧

A bit like robbery or rape, the beekeepers' work,
and a bit like dance, slow, so as not to stir the bees.
The hive is the body their arms encircle,
a cone shape, squirming inside like a pig.
To take the honey, they plant both feet firmly,
tuck the buzzing cone between the legs, and
with claw-like fingers—or are they more like roots—
pry open the lid. There's little chance of feeling
stings through their enormous, padded shoulders.
Afterward, the hive is left lurched in the grass.

❧

Like love. On the losing side you take on the armor of hemp.
You must agree losing something sweet could wreck
a face and turn it into unreadable flatness.
                              The world,
too, turns flat. Somewhere, even now, in a field,
a couple with one body jerks and moans,
as indivisible as honey from a comb.

❧

Then one stands up and one becomes two. And one
by one the two walk in opposite directions
home. One might say change is good; one, that
it's lonely. For bees and keepers, parting,
or its effort, is sticky, hard to do without
protection. Do you hide from the face you sting?
Or, stung, wear a basket? But how to breathe
through that tight cover? How to love what you see?

Mrs. Heinike and Mr. Mendelssohn

"If you would, Mrs. Heinike," Mr. Mendelssohn said
to me at 79 (formerly 103) Great Portland Street in London,
"please keep a cold pudding for me in my living room cupboard."
He liked my kidney pies, too.
"He would lift the crust," my Mr. Heinike always said,
"and was tickled when the juice bubbled up!"

Did you know Mr. Mendelssohn kept two pianos in his rooms?
And a keyboard for his knees; in bed, he shut
his eyes to hear and played. Not a surprise, what
you'd expect of the great, the need to practice,
practice. For just look how a cook must work
to get things right. How many yolks separated,

how many cups of flour & treacle measured,
how many spins of the sifter and spoon before
she can get her kettle pudding great enough
to tickle a Mr. Mendelssohn. *Genius, pure genius,*
perhaps he said, I hope he said, opening the cupboard
at midnight, slipping his lonely spoon in. *Unforgettable.*

Dog Days in Court, 1780's
    —a conversation between Frederick the Great's dog and his sister Wilhelmina's

Then Berlin

Though this letter be clearly written
in my mistress's hand, let it be known, I,

Biche, send you this history, Folichon,
recording the past, including our doghood

in Berlin, when we hid with them,
our masters, in the armoire and

your master Frederick comforted mine
under the odor of old robes.

*Don't worry, Mina, Father will die
some day, and then I'll be king.*

Your Frederick, nurturing two passions,
war and music. He disgusted his father

with his flute-playing. And my Mina
disgusted him with our presence.

As did the Queen. None of us knew
where in the palace she hid.

My Arrival in Bayreuth

In Bayreuth drunks threw up
civilly in corners, not on Mina's dinner

plate. They talked French, took tea
among the villa's tatters. Mina the bride

yearned for panes in windows, bed
hangings to keep drafts out, a table

and a chair. I, shivering, panted to see
your dear face again, and just once, not

a bone, but a bon bon to gnaw on.
Such a marriage, Mina's, bittersweet

as coffee and wild cherries.
How sweet to possess, Folichon!

Not that I'm a hedonist, but, oh!
for a hunk of braunschweiger from Berlin.

The New Margravine's Reign

To celebrate the death of the old Margrave,
an era of frayed cuffs, Mina lit candles to him,

shocking her Protestant subjects
with extravagance, light and import,

evening salons, lively conversations
with Voltaire (who stepped on my toes).

While I sniffed the garden paths,
Mina fired her husband's mistress,

a Prussian, Miss von Marwitz—
never a tidbit from that hand!—

and curbed faux intellectuals
in her park's new Temple of Silence.

Betrayal

Yes, I know Mina allowed the editorial
backing your master's rival,

the Empress. Yes, I know
it was no tail-wagging time;

your Frederick circled his palace
raving. The Empress

being Catholic, Austrian and worst,
a woman. *The bloody, filthy rag.*

Printed in your duchy. How could you, Mina?
Father's laughing in his grave.

Mina and I shuddered over his letter.
A grotesquerie.

As in, *Father will die some day,*
and then I'll be king.

Aftermath, Enduring Love

My dear, divine sister. Frederick's
reconciliation with Mina was ashen,

(foretold by us in letters). Dear Folichon,
berries redden here in Mina's gardens,

her carousel of light and sound is fading.
I forgive your master's teary rage,

gorging on Europe to fatten Prussia.
In this dozing Duchy of Bayreuth,

I accept your sweet paw in marriage
and vow my love till death. Your Biche.

On Brothers: A Conversation Between Dorothy Wordsworth and Nannerl Mozart in the Afterlife

Mozart: It's an airy thing, gloating
over names Wolfgang
used to call me, *Horseface,
My Liver, My Stomach, My Lungs.*

Wordsworth: I was my brother's beloved.
He called me his Beloved.

Mozart: Names keep a place for us
on earth. In church books.

Wordsworth: He rested his head on my shoulder.

Mozart: Have you never traveled alone?

Wordsworth: Only in death.

Mozart: I play to my ghosts forever,
my martyrs to music, to Vienna,
to the carousel of events
on the Empress' calendar.

Wordsworth: William sang, "Oh, my dear, dear sister,
with what transport shall I again meet you."
With the transport of Angel Wings, William!
On the transports of hope, I follow you.

Mozart: Wolfgang always said
the human voice is the greatest instrument.

Wordsworth: Newsprint? I stuffed it
in our window cracks.

Mozart: Mice. Mice pestered Wolfgang in Vienna,
in his apart-from-us.

Wordsworth: I slept with his children to be near William.
I put down their upsets.

Mozart: I know the banishment of attics.
The nicks on the walls. The markers.

Wordsworth: (leaning close) Do you hear your brother's voice?
I hear mine in every line in my journal.

Mozart: I hear house as love.

Wordsworth: Oh, my lines flew
in rags and tatters,
but on Sundays
we fed on rapture,
on Mondays, bliss.

Mozart: *O Cara Armonia.*

Wordsworth: It was given William to write the sacred.
I was given ears, hands and eyes
to copy

Mozart: to play!

Wordsworth: what he wrote.

Mozart: What he wrote.
I do understand. We so anticipate

Wordsworth: his thoughts and moods

Mozart: we wind up quite unable

Wordsworth: to belong to ours. (laughing)
I'm not thankless!
My two years at Grasmere with William bloomed.
My life's complete happiness.

Mozart: Sometimes music, too, can be a small box.

Music, I Must Have Music
    — for the daughters of J.S. Bach: Catharina Dorothea, Elisabeth Juliana, Johanna Carolina and Regina Susanna

"Music, I must have music," you sang, stealing
to clavichords, the seven in the parlor,
seven, never enough, your seven brothers
were quite quick to lay their claim.

But where would Bach have put eleven
in his house? Its music clutter
across the bridge from Zimmermann's,
a coffeehouse for music-loving amateurs.

Over the brook you stole, singing, a flock
of larks, a clatter of cups, one quick jump
from Zimmermann's tables to his clavier—
your father's calling—you, your romping

Musik, Musik, Musik muss ich haben,
splashing in it, *"I must have it,"*
laughing over it, "I must." Your father's
calling you.   Ah, there you go,

stealing away to the fountain, claiming
to be like regular girls in St. Thomas Square,
toting the family's buckets of water home,
letting that clatter spill over your quick steps.

On the Death of His Sister: Goethe's Winter Journey

He wants no show of grief.
No mirror draped in black.
Let the letter rot on the table.
Let its looped, Gothic script swim
away from his eyes. He will not read it
again:

"The sixteenth of June, 1777.
The young Frau Schlosser . . . dead after giving birth."

He will not think it again. *Cornelia,*
the playwright, the bride, the corpse.

He will carouse.
Shoot fireworks in the morning.
To hell with the garden, the grafting.
She is not dead. No!

He'll abandon blue noses, the cottage
on the banks of the Ilm, hours
shucking peas in the courtyard with the women.

Out. Get out. Hike
through the Harz, get brown
under the Continent's sun.
Gone, she is gone. Cornelia.

Why search the Harzland's mine shafts?
Why spend the fall staring
into the iron-founder's flames?
Why mouth her name?

The summit he wanders sleeps
under two-meters snow.
Now he can see.

The cortège of blackpine.
The white face
raw in December mist.

The acute
silence.

"Dear Little Sister"—Wil van Gogh

She is at home in a corner,
a witness to black roosters pecking
it out—Father and brother—flying
right at each other's eye, a raw

defense. *Why don't you leave,
Vincent?* she whispers. *Go.
Assimilate in the Bournasage
the browns in shadow and potato.*

She, the nurse, paints in yellow
light awash in orange-blue.
It's in her blood, too, Vincent's
blue danger. She has that eye, too.

The patient she cares for is calling,
drowning the placid Dutch sky
and apple branch blossom in gray.
Sometimes she wishes she had no ears.

Wonder Woman at Seventy
   —for The Two Fat Ladies

No longer fitting into her hourglass costume—
valentine top and bottom—Wonder Woman
trades her bullet-proof bracelets for a decent
lime squeezer and dons a smock in the kitchen.
Things don't die, only change.

Like "garlic and ginger, a lovely mixture"
improves a cut of meat. Ditto "beloved rosemary,"
tucked under leg of lamb. The ending will be delicious.
All nettles extracted, all artichokes rubbed
with lemon so their tongues won't blacken.

Like God, Wonder Woman has very few vices:
The garlic, the rosemary, a tall glass of gin,
bacon, laid in union-jack strips over an otherwise
dry hen. Rule Britannia! Just pop into the oven.
The bird begins, throatily, to sing.

The Bird Men
    —for *Sterchens,* Katherine Wright, Orv and Wilbur's sister

This thing of being bird-like, weighing
only fifty-two pounds: Their first glider
cost $15.00, a fortune spent on the uncertain.

This thing of dreaming, like seabirds
on the wing, measuring wing spread,
multiplying it by six, both fore and aft

dimension, lateral surface not less,
not more than twenty. Small angles
best for efficiency. This bird-like act

henpecking every technique
for its truth, arched in a warp,
waiting for the right tap, the right twist—

what is crucial, equilibrium, preserved,
flying from gravity without gyrating
into the galaxy of obscurity. This

bird-like flailing, in high wind,
like a buzzard, slow and heavy,
a success that looked like failure.

    ❧

On the shifting sands of Kitty Hawk, on a finger
of sound built up between
the Atlantic and the mainland, on Kill Devil Hills,

in the undomesticated reserve

of Albamarle, the wind
moved air and worry
like furniture around a room.

"Before you can fly, you must glide, Sterchens."

"Wilbur, Orv!
if you need to sew the wing, I'll show you how,
so you can sew it yourself."

II. Home

Wax Cylinder Recordings: Riffs from a Small Town (7 parts)

1. A Shirt to Wear

She rode into town, ignoring the warnings. *Streets, blocked; traffic, uncertain. Ice on the Missouri, thinning.*

She had my sister down under her apron. She didn't know, not at all, the Deloria Sisters from across the river,

the reservation where they buried Sacajawea, hunting grounds for Episcopalians. Ella Deloria

wrote a history of the Sun Dance; her sister Susan preserved a Ghost Dance shirt, made holy

by the massacre at Wounded Knee. It was old muslin, frailer than a tea towel, the designs, worn

as a voice on a wax cylinder recording, magic coming over waves of misfortune.

She didn't know this down in the basement, sorting piles of whites and coloreds to wash.

Chipping away at a cake of lye, she couldn't detect art work in workshirts, stiff with unblessed sweat.

2. Did You Hear That?

The ultimate, airy banister for small things— a canister zipping down a pneumatic tube

from the mezzanine—wheee!—to the main floor in J.C. Penney's, carrying money to a clerk,

who never noticed her own hands, precise, ringing up a sale, say, a prom dress. She

withheld her opinion on how much you spent.
Started working at Penney's in the Twenties,

had to; still on her feet in the Fifties,
Sixties, Seventies. About her, the darkly sweet

fragrance of the weary. A company woman.
She covered her mouth when she coughed,

lower case coughs,
small as the 'c' in scraping by.

3. Response to "Letters to the Editor," Found Poem

"What difference does it make
if we/ *Tribune* misspelled Sakajawea . . .

we shall now call her Bird Woman . . .
she may also be called Mrs. Charbonneau

with a considerable degree
of propriety . . . this means less

wear and tear on our spelling,
enunciation and pronunciation

apparatus, as well as upon the delicate
mechanism of our linotype

machine and the nervous system
of its patient, long-suffering operator."

4. The Sixth District Women's Convention

She thumbed her nose at the ladies
from her washer in the basement.

She was as pretty, and surely as quick
as an Honorable Mention, and at times,

as desperate as the ladies for something
other than dust, but she'd married

a peasant. Handsome, but sorry, wrong
class—as if she were interested

in lawyered, doctored, business-manned
wives. As if she wanted to join their clubs,

the *Cultus*, the *L'Eclatant Douzaine,*
chicken-saladed, pink-tableclothed

gatherings. As if she wanted to listen
to Mrs. Cott's "My Trip to Rothenburg,"

or hear some heavy-chested canary
warble Wagner. His *Dämmerung.*

5. Drive

The new woman drove, unlike my mother.
A free woman like Maude Caldwell, owner

of one of the town's first five automobiles;
free to keep her first name after "Mrs.," have accidents,

leave town, spend the winters in Minneapolis.
Maude did perms. If the client's husband

was short of cash, he could work off the cost
in or outside the shop, a place

so small when Maude did Mrs. Batteen's
river of hair, she had to keep swaying

back, back into a closet to comb
to the end, the soft, brown waves.

Handsome, willowy Mrs. Batteen,
mistress to the richest man in Walworth County.

Her hair, heavy in Maude's hands, almost as heavy
as her lover's name, engraved on the public

library's lintel. *Never short of cash,
that one*, Maude'd say, as she drove by.

6. I Get Her Name into Print

Ella Grace Clara,
speak from the cellar,

what is your counsel for me?

7. Other Women

Other women worked in a cabin in the willows
along the river, their nipples, targets,

little bombshells for drunken johns
with pistols. Mae West lookalikes,

coming in sweet, Five-and-Ten perfume.
Their scarlet lipstick planted untidy O's

on married men's collars. (One stain
led to another to be washed in the cellar

with work shirts, slow to take offense.)
After the town routed out the West End,

whores scattered like cats down alleys,
so mangy they became police notes

in the *Tribune*, under the rung where
the poor, approved by the County for relief,

clustered in chillblained lists. I could go on,
but you see. The past falls, like a descant

from Eden. Voices get lost. Mrs. Bachelor,
our kitty-corner neighbor, whose kitchen

shone cloud-white, told my mother, "Ella,
heaven and hell are right here on earth."

In Each Other's Hair

This took place long ago on a strip of lawn:
The seed blown in from who knows where,
for free. We needed rags (for curls)
so Ma ripped up a dish towel, embroidered
muslin. My sister carried out the stool,
wooden, handmade for the kitchen. The dry,
summer, endless sky favored no one
below it though I was promised I'd be
beautiful. I brought my wet-haired self
and sat; behind me Ma unsnarled and wrapped
my hair for locks. But it was the doing,
the going out beyond walls,
a caravan of three, bearing throne
and wrapping, comb and jar of summer
myrrh and hairpins. We set up camp
among lilacs, beside a bed of dusty mint.
Nothing of the afternoon was expected
to remain, not the tending nor the laughing,
nor the cups of love spent carelessly, as if it were
water and we lived in the shadows of a stream.

Lucifer at the Supper Table

> . . . from Morn to Noon he fell, from Noon to dewy Eve,
> A Summer's day; and with the setting Sun Dropt
> from the Zenith like a falling Star . . .
> Milton, *Paradise Lost*

. . . and is sitting at my mother's table.
He has hung his hat on the corner of the door,
open to the breeze, "the breece,"
the porch door open to cool things down.

He eats like a German, mid-arms resting
on the table, spills nothing on his chin.
Should a pea roll from his plate, he bends
to pick it up, hemming himself into the tiny

kingdom he has landed in, our land
of stove, land of table, of big chair and radio,
four corners that can't accommodate
the spread of his wings; the dizzying

ivy wallpaper, fit only for a fly.
Our offerings, a platter of cold cuts.
He's handsome, my fallen father, looking
out the photo's frame as I am looking

in. We are as small as dolls,
the furniture has shrunk. His is the only
face that looks up from the table. His,
the only smile. It could be threatening. Or broken.

Milton on the Plains: the Coal Furnace

> A Dungeon horrible, on all sides round
> As one great Furnance flam'd, yet from those flames
> No light, but rather darkness visible
> Serv'd only to discover sights of woe. . .
> —*Paradise Lost*

Like Milton's ours burned with unholy light.
My parents fed it in our basement's dusk,
two shadows banking darkness. Mom in gloves
and housedress, would heft a shovelful of lignite
to horrid lips and shove it in. Then clang!
The iron firing door slammed shut. Upstairs,
we walked the floorboards hearing smoldering coal;
trip on a floor vent, the fall burned like hell.
Imagination's fuel. A dose of Poe
ignites the tale: a heart that's ripped in two,
a night of drunken fury, a man who feeds
his wife to fire, limb by bloodied limb.
And who would stop her husband's deeds of woe?
His children? Hell's walls hold in the screams.
No one can search its ashy pit for bones.
The devil's throbbing anthem rings, *Forever
together.*
        I prayed for a deliverer,
someone to tame the furnace, seal it up.
Hammer racket would convert it
to lighter gas or oil, a furnace fed
by tubes no man could shove a body through.

McIntosh, South Dakota

Outside the four-room house with porch and buckled walk,
a car pulls up on this Sunday noon, a Chevy, a '48 or '49.
The doors swing open; a man, woman and child in braids slide out.
The woman still young enough to have all her own teeth.
It's 1950 or '52, I'm guessing, for this isn't a photo, but memory,
not in sepia, but in gray. As for the jolly woman on the porch,

she's the man's aunt, beaming. His uncle, Fred, on the step,
operated a threshing rig with the man's father in the Antelope Valley,
before Fred became a heretic, got his worship day all screwed up,
turned Seventh Day Adventist, was banished from North Dakota
to Canada, Saskatchewan's wheat fields, then South Dakota's and now
his belly shows who sits in the living room waiting for dinner.

The aunt is wiping her hands on her starched and ironed apron.
The uncle extends his hand. Come in, come in, *Herein!*
The table is an offering, the bounty of reconciliation. First, steaming
soup, homemade noodles. Then mashed potatoes, beef, pickles,
garden lettuce drowned in cream, crust-cracking bread and kuchen,
heavy on whole cream, eggs and butter. Conflagrations of fragrance:

The onus is on the child; of the five, sweating over their plates
of forgiveness, she will live longest. She's handicapped: she hasn't
the vaguest notion how anything is driven or made from scratch.
To her, things just are. She isn't even aware of her job, to hold
the memory as close as heaven, a history where they'll live forever,
warm and out-moded. A gray sort of comfort she'll find in the lost.

Now It's Late

afternoon, rain runs down the folds in the plastic awning
over the front step. Conversation's left for its holy house,
quietly closed the door, following a path love made long ago.
Or was it duty? House clocks tick, the cuckoo, a beat ahead
of the grandfather. Four ticks to each ha-rumpf.
May air dozes in the living room after dinner
with a man and woman, fallen asleep sitting up.
The man's hands lie open on his leg and armrest,
great, wide paws, felled by sleep.
He nods defenseless, his head, a pompadour under snow.
The woman sits in her green-padded rocker,
her head slumped on her chest, gasping, now and then,
as though someone's just stuck her with a pin.
She almost leaves sleep but drifts back down again
to rest in the parlor of the sleeping kingdom.
Angers lie about, old smoke still adrift over the carpet.
Blame has curled up, its head on the sofa's pillow, its face
young again in sleep. Where's the prince who must come
to kiss old lips? Maybe he's fallen short of reaching the door.
He and his horse, under the spell; the house, unwakeable.

Fruit Closet

Is it right to spend one's time dwelling
on an old fruit closet and its door handle
(a homemade cross-bar holding two doors
from flapping open, swinging out)? Is it wise?
To want to remember, keeping it just as was,
like something rich, but, really, an awkward
armoire, painted 1920 movie star green,
thin-walled, made by a father, its shelves
two and one-half feet deep, a sturdy box,
set off the earth floor on wooden blocks.
By summer's end, a storehold gleaming
with jars, specimens under glass, skinned
pears, peaches, crabapples, sweetened
for the winter table. "Take home more,"
my father moans after my mother's death.
"I can never eat all of it up."
Chokecherries, tomatoes, rhubarb, plums,
cherries, jams, jellies, spiked by the inevitable
bad jar that popped in the back. Spewed
its fumes. (She could've put her foot down.
She could have turned from the sink
when he towered into the kitchen with his
bulging handful of tomatoes, beginning
the canning season. "Why continue this?"
she could have said. "We will never eat this
down. The past is already too full.")
Canning is a historical act, once common
and cyclical, performed by my mother's hands,
which neither death nor new ways changed;
they were the only part of her that looked
real before the lid was closed.

III. Behind the Curtain

Pictures From an Extinction: The Motherland

On the outskirts of Chernobyl,
the house of an old woman,
her father gave it to her
as his mother gave it to him,
the same wardrobe and same sofa,
the same embroidered cloth
—red and czarist—over the table;
in the middle, the same bowl,
veined gloom and hunger
in late afternoon.

Tree in the garden,
a hologram, a statue,
a white incineration.

A chain of people circle the tree.
They can't stop themselves from stripping
its harvest. A moth-and-spider-gauze
sticks to their fingers and lips.
They devour the apple flesh, spitting out
brown states of seeds.
The earth writhes. How these people
hate their treasonous stomach.
Its groaning, churring satisfaction
with juice and corrupt pulp,
as if they'd fed it something
they could live from.

It's the end of the world,
half the people live
in Paradise. The other half,
ash. It's the end
of a word, end of mercy.
Zeus technology
pardons no human mistake.

Remember Jehovah the judge,
Siamese twins?
On the one hand casting
us out of Eden?
Even while his better half
prepared a table for us
in the presence of our enemies?
    ❧

The leukemia ward in Kiev,
a former palace, has these
wonderful European windows,
glass cupboard doors
the nurse unlatches.

Children, in rows
of white beds,
direct little wings
of fright in their eyes
toward the opened wall.
    ❧
Tree of life,
menorah branches.
Apples and leaves,
red and green threats.
In a white garden
the watchman's gone blind.
    ❧
The old woman again,
reflected in her window,
a pose of eating;
supper, a collage on glass:
Scarfed head, the table's
midland, its cracked bowl,
the spoon in swollen hand—
whatever it yields,
steaming.

Three Faces
—from Katherins Turczan's "Portraits from Ukraine"

I see you, Jesus, in your sweet,
boy-mobster disguise, crowned by
the available fox tail and canary grass wreath.

Nothing else, besides your bared,
bony chest, resurrected. The future,
in unenviable shoes, has come to kiss you.

What are you offering us now?
A gray angel to sit on our bed?
He's no comfort to the pregnant

young woman. His wings, stubs,
a lover fallen from heaven. A stud.
Soon with another mouth to feed.

This can be as frightening as your bride,
Jesus, a sixty-year-old virgin,
hardened folds in her unkissed cheeks,

smug as her black, clump-heeled shoes,
fixed to the convent floor. Her curtains,
always white. Her lamp, filled with oil.

Not like Antonia, the black-market
butcher, whose hands are lard-white
from working in flesh and blood.

Akhmatova's Place

Ascending and descending,
a condition of survival,
outbluffing doors
that open to another
closed door.

Walking, seeing
everything in a rush,
while seeing nothing.
Hearing the void.
Feeling it.

Not hopeful, not
hopeless. Haggard.
Gray as the Fontanka's waves.
Her thoughts kept
behind a forehead

in the city's pretty
heart, her
crushing home,
her eyes'
hooded domain.

Stalin's Daughter
    —or: Who poisoned Stalin?

He orders by pointing—that man's sausage,
that woman's bread. I order the vegetable,
potatoes. "What's a matter," he says
across the table, "you on a diet?
Take my advice, eat. Fat on your bones
is healthy. You never know when
you'll need it." He rips his bread apart,
sops up the plate's grease, dabs fat
from his mustache, then eats
the sweet rag, chases it down
with a shot. He wipes his lips
with the back of his hand. His belch,
soft, like a cat's, jars only his shoulders.
"I don't care," he says, "what those bastard
doctors say. What do they know!"
I take a packet from my purse, God forgive me,
slide its little drawer open, offer him
what looks like a licorice. Smiling,
he presses the black spot to his tongue.

A Christmas Story . . . of a Sort

For behold, Erika's Christmas cactus blooms again,
long after her death and its journey to our house
from her apartment where the cactus flourished
in the room's desert air, the way some refugees
cross borders like years, arriving at a window
after a long, dark spell on a re-named street,

in denial of the room landed in, a firetrap
of cords, some snaking up a wall, some,
creeping along a baseboard; one, taped
to a table leg. On a hanger, a coquettish
white slip clung to the gray seersucker suit
found in the bundle from a rummage sale.

"I was frivolous once," Erika sighed as if
time were fragrant, or water, sipped from a china
cup in the German academy in St. Petersburg.
Oh, to stay in 1912. Decades before a stroke
did her in, before the world stood her up,
turned frivolous twit into *Putzfrau*, arched-nosed

bearer of an American rest home's shit pans.
So who would have thought after a long,
silent exile, a flowering would return
to Erika's cactus with such éclat? Risen
on stems, dry as Jesse's root, belting out
protest at any absence of light in the world.

The Bürgermeister's Wife's Account: Salzburg, 1750

She was sixteen years old when she took to the woods
near her parents' farm, couldn't get along, wouldn't work.
Let her go, I said, she'll tire of stuffing straw in rags for shoes.
Her mother had her carted off to the Rathaus,
had her put in stocks and branded "thief."
The Bürgermeister gave any man on horseback
leave to whip her. Still she thumbed her nose.
Let her eat snow, I said. Who was she after all?
A *Tunichtgut.* Not the kind of woman you'd want
playing clavier while you played violin or brushing
your hair as you watched in the mirror. She was
a liar, lighting fires and showing the between-
her-legs to dogs though she swore she never
swapped the fagot bundle for the dead baby.
No man could have been more filthy-mouthed.
We washed hers out good once, in the Salzach.
And her hole. Dirtier than a pig she was, rutting
in an alley with any man for a crust, both his poker
and her hole greasy as the cobbles they did it on.
Her hair, a vipers' nest. You'd be sitting in the inn,
her face would appear, nose pressed to the window,
a smear of mucus and curse. She was without doubt
hopeless. From her no prince of the Church would
ever collect a single tax. She was easy to push
toward the block; she was as content as the old to go.
When they drew the sword over her head, she laughed.
She was happy when the blade fell.   She was.

The Last Queen of France

At some point opulence becomes obscene.
The fish on the table, a forkful of flesh,
once delicious, turns into jaded gangrene.

The rest? Amaze me, amaze, amaze.
Think use of alcohol. Weed. Fame. Main
character, the Queen. Taken from mother

tongue, hers is inadequate, no vessel
for the gush, the desired French;
fluency gets stuck in a child's syntax.

A ragged audience waits outside the palace,
ready to stuff its belly at her tables,
and after heaving, purge the Queen's

lovely, rapacious mouth from its gorging.
A head for bread, the barter system;
a whole life, halved. Extreme unction.

A body feels lighter that way. Delicate.
The guillotine, a simple palliative.
For even at the Queen's plainest—

a garden with meadow stream, ox-eyes,
cosmos and butterflies—there was that
distasteful abundance of prettiness.

Jephthah's Daughter

> If thou shalt without fail deliver the children of Ammon into mine hands, then shall it be that whatsoever cometh forth of the doors of my house to meet me when I return . . . shall surely be the Lord's and I will offer it up for a burnt offering. (Judges 11: 30-31)

I danced to the Arnon and the Jabbok,
to strings I liked best, harp and lyre,
to timbrel and tambourine, too;
they made the blood rise.
God saw me, and He was pleased,
giving victory to my father, the Captain.

Then we watched, my friends and I,
from the rooftop. We saw my father
leading his army, waves of men
flooding back across the plains.
The old, faithful servants circled,
ululating like locusts. I danced

to the door. What did he expect
would meet him? A goat?
A servant, yawning, stumbling
into morning? A foot soldier,
dying at the gate, too wounded
to reach home? Who was his only child?

Oh daughter, he cried out,
you've been a very great trouble.
He lifted his arms, rent his robe
soaked with the stench of battlefield.
Whatsoever cometh forth.
I couldn't breathe.

I dressed in white for the altar,
white for the priest. I offered
my name to the forever, whatsoever.
The priest's knife flashed then,
and hot, thick, my blood
danced on my father's lips.

Burning

> . . . I don't want to be burned.
>
> Louise Glück, *Averno*

Ah, but I want to burn, the way the field, the strong field,

the known field is burned in fall and spring in anticipation,

oh, much quicker than the slow clearing of flesh from bone.

Burned, loose from its scaffolding, flesh is a change into light,

into motes, scattering, over field, dust, catching in air, once

every winter I see this play as snow descends on a field

and its field tree, *gloriosa et immaculata,* and the joy

watching that change, I stand in the field by myself. At home.

You had children, I had none, I have no one to show the field,

or tell I'm sorry, or call and ask if they are lonely,

I have something to give nothing; call me a show-off, call me

willing to cut off my nose . . . when it comes, I'm ready to burn,

free of all boxing or packaging, it won't last long, that heat, that

singeing intensity on the flesh and then, the vibrant exit into wind.

IV. And Then, Love

Monet's Egg Girl

I walk through the gardens
to the back door.
Madame isn't ready
with the money, so I
follow her into the dining room.

She keeps her coins in a tin
like we do. I touch
a chair, the table. Once I saw
the moon this color. I run
my hand over the cupboard, its
sunflower brightness. I could hide
one of the plates on the shelf
in my basket. My heart
thumps, let me stay here.

The priest is right. There is an eternity.
A yellow that doesn't go gray.
But Madame Monet, pushing my
shoulders, says it's time for me to leave.

Be too eager, *le père* says, and you'll lose
the job you have now. *La mère* hoots.

In summer my face
is the color of a brown egg;
in winter, white.
I wear a dull gray dress with another
at home just like it for Sunday.

I ask *la mère* if I may have a yellow dress.
She looks at me as if I'm crazy.
Then, a pair of yellow stockings?
Pour la nouvelle année. Je t'en prie.
I've never pleaded with *la mère* before.

I dream yellow. Yolk yellow, without an egg's
stickiness. I dawdle at Monet's windows
as I pass by.

Chickens. Chickens.
I duck out of the hen house,
chicken shit on my shoes.
La mère plucks a feather from my hair.

Today Monsieur Monet says he admires
very much the colors in my banty red rooster's
feathers. And I, as bold as I'll ever be, I say
I adore his yellow dining room.
He doesn't understand. I mean,
Adore. He laughs. You have
good taste, he says, *ma chère* egg girl.

I put my hand to my chest.
My heart is beating hard.
And that is that. And that is that.
The sun in his room.

On the Train to Milan, the Conductor, *il Controllore*

1.
He is not a cheat. Knee to knee in the railroad car,
we balance books on our laps; his, black, mine,
a Berlitz. None of the phrases in it seem to apply;
still, he is kind, too kind, like a father or uncle.
One who knows you cannot set off in a hot, turbulent
world alone without luck as a companion, and that's why,
he sighs, I must pay more. His gestures paw
huge, bosomy surcharges in the air. His face
films with an afternoon of sweat, his voice,
the essence of sadness as he holds out his hand.
Prego, prego. It's a relief, not understanding but
handing over the cash. It could have been so much more;
so many other things gone wrong he could have spotted.
It's enough he's sat down with me, the foreigner.

2.
He's too kind to be a good lover
or cheater. His knee bones pull
on his trousers' twill, creased,
like his face; if he washed it,
he might feel better. He leans
forward, his hands sweating.
What I understand is the sadness
in his outstretched hand.
What I understand is that
essence of happiness in giving
him, of all men, my money.

3.
What is a small price to pay for dear, underpaid tenderness?
Twenty, thirty lire? To have a man on a train sit down
beside you? *Il controllore* is not a cheat. He balances
his intentions with his duties, listed in the black book
on his lap. I pull out my Berlitz. I'm alone, an illiterate
in Italian, already two counts against me. I understand
his brown collie eyes. *Prego, Prego.* I understand he'll stay
as long as necessary. I understand I'm lucky I can pay.

4.
Poor man. So upset. Trying so hard,
and I don't understand one word
he's saying, sighing, *Prego, prego,*
poring over his black, opened book.

5.
You must go out expecting to run into
all kinds of weather. You must try to
understand just because you are alone
and can read, somewhat, *il controllore's*
upset face, his brown, drowning eyes,
the opposite of happiness, his gestures
and words go up in flame whether
the source is understood or not.
For you are in *il controllore's* section,
and he is nodding over your opened
purse, taking what he wants, and now,
Signora! Triumphant! He'll lead you
over the next hundred kilometers of future.

6.
How is it, a woman will sit alone,
a woman of a certain age, and no one
will see her? She looks out the train window.
Il controllore comes along, he in his once
handsome blue uniform. He with his cap.
His black book and scuffed shoes. He
is the one who sits down beside her. *Prego!*
He tries to explain in his language,
which she doesn't understand, nor he, hers,
why he sat down. The woman—of great
imagination—smiles at all the reasons
of the heart that could be. None are his.
His, he explains, opening the black book
on his lap, his is a matter of surcharge.
So! There it is, like a pratfall: a matter
of money.
            Which she pays.

The Islanders

        Why you come, and not expect to pay?
        Sir.
        Eat your *Harpers*.

The useless pay for the taxi man's third ear.
And the gas.
And the chicken in his pot.
He want it.
He campaign for it.
He say yes! over the steering wheel,
"You fix it for me tonight."
Bang. He hang up.
He stop by the store
right after the useless
pay their fare and get out.

      ❧

The soul is very deep.
Yes, the soul is deep.
Hard to walk on.
Harder maybe than snow.
And not so clean.
All kinds of things
wash up on it
from that ocean,
things that smell old.

      ❧

You take Myrtle now.
You take Myrtle who smells
like a branch of myrtle.
You take Myrtle who does
the laundry, she stuck down there
in the big room, hot, no windows
down there with all those carts
and tubs and dryers.
That's business.
That's the business.
Good Business. Myrtle,
rolling the big vat of dirty bedclothes.

"You stay out of sight!"
That Myrtle can glare at those kids.
One fat, one skinny.
Kind of shy and happy.
Sweet. Not angry
like their Mommy,
Myrtle. Yet.
       ॐ
Snipping the rhododendrum hedge.
Snip snip.
Trimming the rhododendrum hedge.
Trim trim.
Don't wanna snip. Don't wanna trim.
Snip snip.
       ॐ
Black butterfly.
Black butterfly aflutter
over the bougainvillea.
Black business going on
up in the night sky.
Ocean going black, too.
Black going way out into
the universe's middle.
All fear and sugar.
       ॐ
Don't start talking now to the women.
You leave them alone.
Those clouds mean nothing.
Those clouds blow over.
Sun going blast again.
Don't start talking with the women.
They going help you to your room.
They going get you your fresh towels.
They going bring you a fresh drink.
They got their friends at home.
Don't start talking now to the women.
You got the clouds.

❧

Banana milk. 1% low fat.
U.S. dollar a carton.
Paper cartons that picture
bright yellow bananas.
Creamy banana milk inside.
Straight from the banana's
tit. Mmmm, good. I go for it.
I stop by every morning and
buy a banana milk from the lady.
Cool lady. Cool, brown lady.
Cool banana milk.
Straight from her cooler.
I drink it right there in her store,
on the spot. She works there
but lives with her mama and daddy.
She don't work on Sunday.
"Why they expect me to work on Sunday?
I got washing to do.
I got some living to do.
I got to rest up for opening the store
door on Monday. Let you in."

❧

I saw clouds the other day.
I saw clouds, piling up gray,
streaming down all over from the north.
I saw clouds and thought it surely would rain.
I didn't expect snow.
I surely didn't expect snow here.
Snow clogging up the sky,
spoiling the breakfast mood.
No one called for snow
falling over everything.

❧

Now why would someone say a sax
is like an oboe? Wouldn't you think
that woman would recognize a sax?
Maybe she was thinking of the fingering.
But that's way different, too.

She got the mouth thing right—
the embouchure.
If you have full lips you have
to tuck them in to pipe that little
thin reed. Well, I left her
and went on to my temp job.
I left him, too, I left him and went on
to taking care of a rich woman's roses.
Her tables full of vases of roses.
Some, dry like her husband.
He come out into the kitchen.
I told him why I was there in his house,
I could tell his lip was working hard to trust me.
Those roses were beautiful though.
Those roses were just beautiful.
Almost like a city. You never saw
such roses as that rich lady's.
You never touched such rich velvet
as on those petals. Those roses sang!
Some other people looking in
on me in her house, too.
They didn't recognize me either.
I could have been a sax or clarinet or oboe.

View from Porch

Last week a storm took down an apple tree,
its shade over the porch
from the western sun,
and its bonus, apples.
It left behind space to see
to the very end of the yard.

There, clearly, The Little House sits.
An innocent face of corner windows,
side door, bordered by lilies and mint.
My sister's first house when she married.
Now it's summer kitchen and storage.
It could be more but isn't.

She's clearing it out slowly, an act,
I think, of unnecessary hastening,
to spare her daughter the final cleaning.
Masses of hollyhocks, brown-eyed Susans,
moss roses and petunias volunteer
to brighten the unused, gravel driveway.

The sweetest of morning breezes
blows through the porch screens.
We eat a light breakfast, like ladies,
at a table painted cheery yellow.
The wind chime shivers. "It feels
like fall," my sister breathes.

We sweep away the lengthening
shadows, their wintry signs,
into one of mind's back corners,
preferring to stay in morning,
its own screened walls calling,
"Come in and abide all summer."

Mr. Schmier's Wife

was champion of high-rising potato bread.
Her bosom, big as baskets under her apron.

She kept her parlor cool and neat.
At her fingertips, *National Geographics*

offered a variety of continents
and women, some with proud,

plate lips, some with long,
vase-like necks, some with breasts,

mahogany cups, perfectly tipped.
But what Mr. Schmier's wife

liked best was the little stoves
those women baked round breads in.

Red, Red Rose; a Loose, Loose Story

She almost nodded off behind the wheel.
It was that kind of dread, that attar
of roses in the back seat, roses
a student gave her, a swelling red.

They'd met in a garden, and he'd
picked an armful of red. Her heart,
quickened at his touch, it almost
fell in love with him. Almost.

Danger, post classroom danger.
She craved it like sweet sleep,
a Morpheus, eight thousand
years old and still going strong.

And she so modern, her thinking,
so modern, driving about in her broil
red car which she didn't want to smash.
No, she really didn't, it was her bull

in the china shop, the size
of her little heart. Things so
smashed there, so irretrievably
broken at this point. A grave, oh,

say, condition, since she loved to drive,
but mustn't close her eyes, no, couldn't drive
asleep with the scent of roses, waxing
very big in the back seat and waxing.

V. Galileo's Daughter

Sister Maria Celeste (a poem in fourteen sayings)

Money Solves Most Problems

                    If one has it,
one can buy any sacrifice on earth.
Galileo's daughters, two blood sisters
dropped off at the gate to the convent,
are ushered in by money; it buys their future.
And pomegranate and aloe, bread
when sisters are starving, a pad
for their cold stomachs when the abbess,
la Madonna, determines the blankets must
be gathered for storage, despite a freakish
return to cold weather.
                    Only innocents
think confinement and a change of names—
from Virginia to Suor Maria Celeste, from
Livia to Suor Arcangela—come for free.

The Heavenly Father Sends Our Earthly Father to Love Us

At last Suor Celeste has a cell to herself.
No more nights sleeping with four sisters.

Sire, her father, found the money to buy quiet.
She had only the pittance she receives as pay.

How she regrets the seven hours' sleep
her body demands. In that luxury,

oblivion and dreams, the sisters of San Matteo
barely drift. Lord knows

why their poverty helps the world.
Villagers believe the sisters' prayers

are especially heard. Seeing the state
of her heart, Suor Celeste prays for sugar,

to bind its sender to its receiver,
in this otherwise miserable world.

Earth Offers Us a Taste of Heaven

I live in this miserable world of lovely places.
The convent's orchard, the fading sunlight
beams through the refectory window at dusk,
ambering the table and chairs' wood.
Mornings in fall, the peasants' lane,
leading to fields bordered by cypress,
falls soft underfoot, the dew dark against
a lavender sky and orange-veiled meadow.
In the chapel I love the tabernacle
door's click. I caress Holy Mary's arm,
smoothed travertine. Oh. No colder than mine.

It Is No Wonder the Poor Are Poor in Spirit

Galileo's little mule,
a beast of burden,

hired out and badly mistreated,
a sweet, faithful, four-legged menial

led by Geppo, makes a six-legged duo,
born to convey parcels and letters

to and from Galileo's daughter.
Homesick for its master,

and confused by human borders,
the ass brays its strange song,

defenseless and invisible, known
to the martyred, other world.

The Seasons Go Round in Order

The citron sweetening in its season
she candies for her father. The rule
she follows turns from wine to vinegar.

She turns the cloth that makes the collar,
makes soap for a collar's washing.
The tears she finds and mends—

her slender fingers stitching, working,
moving as threads in a fugue—are gaps

as raggedly loose in the world
as her Sire's ideas. As if this planet
could be circled by the sun! Fixed.

A savior. A knot is made; thread,
snapped. The fact is stitched:
Sun will never bow to earth: Proof

are the dark-robed planets in Rome,
genuflecting on their axis, circling
Il Papa's golden throne, kissing his ring.

Both daughter and father accept this
denigration, as order in the seasons.

The Necessity for Wine Can't Be Ignored

Suor Celeste sips it, training her tongue,
with its thirteen-year-old tastes for loving
sweet, abhorring sour, not to cringe.

Unlike her sister Suor Arcangela who
favors the good red wine Sire sends.
Who can trust the water in Tuscany?

During prayer, one doesn't meditate
on Jesus; the water, the blood
can be fraught with disease.

Wine, too, carries its own
chancy cravings. No safety
can be imbibed in this world.

But what is Galileo's daughter doing?
She who should be so busy mending
that I—she—cannot think.

The Heart Is Often Embattled

To fear the Heavenly Father and His rod.
To love the earthly father and his face.

To pray to Him always, hourly.
Mindful of his absence, to correspond daily.

As late as the third hour of the evening,
the wise heart-beat, the watch, the minute

ask blessings from the disciplines He sends.
To know him in your heart and mind and feet.

The path dust knows,
the fermentation in the cask,

recognize the Lord is close.
To adore the path he treads to visit you.

To remember Him always in everything you make.
To care that he not get sick. To care that he is old.

In the apothecary, to prepare pills for his maladies,
saffron for his stomach. Papal pills for headache.

To know everything comes from Him. That blood
drums your love for him each moment.

To thank him for making you in love. (How could he
leave you?) To thank Him for this convent.

Good Wine: It Is But One Remedy for Good Health

The best remedy during pestilence is distance.
The outer door latched. The peep-hole shut.
If she boils the mutton to string, Suor Celeste can get it down.
If she works extra hard, though feeble, she can do the chores
of the nun who lies in bed, ill, unable to raise her head.
If she keeps an eye on the level of wine in the casks,
there's enough at the table to go 'round all winter.
Can the Lord make out the herbalist's small figure
in the garden? Of the convent's flasks, viols, amphora,
she knows. Of herbs and citrons and syrups.
Of poultices and ointments, recipes passed along
by word of mouth. Isn't there always hope?
What evil tongue would speak malice? For what purpose?
That the sick should suffer, that there's no hope?

Lifting Up Your Heart Is Beneficial: Antiphon

As in directing the choir. One of Suor Celeste's chores.
        One that's not paid enough, monthly or daily.
As in singing the music for the Eucharist, Christ's one drama.
        One re-enacted as Mass for our benefit.
As in a holy day, not to be profaned by a priest.
        One unfit to bless the sacraments.
As in a man who's bought the sacred position.
        One with free wine and free pinching.
As in a steady supply because nuns can't run away.
        One terrible, shameful muddle.
As in writing to Galileo, to petition at least the bishop.
        One real priest: Could His Excellence find one for us?
As in a priest who can celebrate the Eucharist.
        One not needing Suor Celeste's prompting.
As in receiving for one's sacrifice more than a jot and tittle.
As in wearing new linen wimples. Oh! One looks quite beautiful.

Love Is the Best War; Armor Yourself with Weapons

Celeste:	Sire likes my nutmeg stomach balm,
Arcangela:	but my rosemary flower jam better!
Both:	Our elixirs. Our roses of sugar for Sire,
Celeste:	who lets not one star go by
Arcangela:	without a letter, sending his best
Celeste:	wines and wishes, a *moggio* of wheat
Arcangela:	and a pair of worn collars
Both:	which we bleach and return.
	We are so entirely in love with him.
Celeste:	Even the charming, yellow kitten
Arcangela:	who found, in the courtyard,
Celeste:	the basket of thrushes Sire sent,
Arcangela:	and ate the top two,
Celeste:	receives our forgiveness.
Both:	Who knows?
Arcangela:	Perhaps *la gattina* liberated the birds
Celeste:	out of the goodness in her heart.

One Sickens of Sickness

Today slowed me down considerably.
My tasks ambled on ahead of me, and I
never really caught up on the path.

Thanks to my pills, and a flask
of Sire's good wine, la Madonna
lies quiet in bed at this time,

after stabbing herself with a knife,
and striking her head against the floor.
We fear her and for her.

I pray for our bad deeds
and secret vices. What evil
could the Holy Mother not dispel

by Her presence? May the procession
carrying the Merciful Virgin on the road
to Florence pass this way soon.

A Small Garden Has the Large Garden's Troubles

This is my mouth, the one which drinks and speaks.
Small you may notice, a small drawer to a cabinet
which is usually quite empty. Hollow.
Only a few teeth left inside that chamber; no matter,
those that are present, ache. I smile behind my hand
at their bounty in my world of repaired clocks.
Sire's clock. His skills are superb at repair.
He must not forget me. Oh, not! Then my life,
already so small, just my sister and I, and
the Almighty, a few dried figs, some meatless soup,
would shrink to nil. Sire sends us a pot
of caviar to fill us up. It does not suit me.
My stomach churns at asking for plainer fare,
for I am always demanding of Sire some favor,
more than my share. I pray for sun and rain.
An equal supply of both; thus the garden's
broad beans and our lemons need not struggle.

Luck Sometimes Occurs Naturally

Suor Angelica is now draper.
She has lost her position of cellarer,
having enjoyed wine too much.
She's now in charge of bleach.

Thanks be to God. At his recent death
the farmer adjacent our convent left
his farm to us, guaranteeing eighty
casks of wine this year, *Morselletti*

from God's table. And if, for Advent,
Sire could find in his orchard a plate
of apricots to send, they'd be met
with the same joy darkness loses to light.

A Mystery Can Never Be Solved

I dwell in prison; left to my own devices,
I must squirm under the load. Can it possibly be
borne on these shoulders? My body the Small.

A thousand years pass before tomorrow comes,
and yet they go by quickly. Light's eye sees in
to my cell. The universe, Sire writes, is our keep.

And yet, I have these kitchen pleasures, making
sweet comestibles at the stove, breathing in deeply their
fruity wisdom and, like my Sire, giving it all away.

Notes

page 3. Subjects: Artemisia Gentileschi, Baroque painter: Her talent was recognized during her lifetime, 1593-1652. She and her painter father often chose harsh subjects from the Bible's early stories for dramatic paintings.

page 9. Dog Days in Court, 1780s: The subject is Wilhelmina, Margravine of Bayreuth, 1709-1758, of the Hohenzollern family and sister to Frederick the Great of Prussia, 1712-1786, a Protestant. Their father the king, when drunk, was a terror in the castle. A few brave servants protected the children from him. Wilhelmina and Frederick named their dogs Biche and Folichon who corresponded by exchanging letters. In this poem, the dogs reflect on their doglife. The Empress mentioned is the Catholic Maria Theresa, a Hapsburg.

page 12. On Brothers: Dorothy Wordsworth: 1771-1855 (died at 84), William Wordsworth: 1770-1850 (died at 80), Nannerl Mozart: 1751-1829 (died at 78, blind) and Wolfgang Mozart: 1756-1791 (died at 35).

page 14. Music, I Must Have Music: Of J.S. Bach's twenty-one children, twelve survived, four of them girls. Three, too musically odd in habits to marry, died in poverty. In *The Bach Family Tree* Father Bach included only his male children.

page 17. "Dear Little Sister" was the endearing salutation Vincent used in letters to his sister. Wil van Gogh was also a painter; also "gifted" with Vincent's madness which, her brother Vincent wrote, "must be looked on as any other disease." Hers was uncomplicated by wine, women, tobacco; she lived longer.

page 18. Wonder Woman at Seventy: The quotations used in this poem come from "Two Fat Ladies," a TV cook show featuring Jennifer Paterson and Clarissa Dickson Wright, who, unfortunately for all her fans, died of cancer.

page 19. The Bird Men: Orville and Wilbur nicknamed Katherine Wright (1874-1929) *Sterchens*, an abbreviated form of *Schwesterchen*, little sister.

page 25. Wax Cylinder Recordings: The idea for this sequence came from the following quotation in the *Mobridge Tribune,* South Dakota, 1920s: "Wanted: Woman, educated, good approach, opportunity to learn good business, must be free to leave the city. . . ." The Deloria Sisters' father was a Lakota Episcopalian priest on Standing Rock Reservation. The title of this book's first section was inspired by the culture clubs mentioned in this poem.

page 42. Akhmatova's Place: Like many Russian poets, Anna Akhmatova, 1889 to 1966, was hounded by Stalin. She died in Soviet Leningrad/St. Petersburg.

page 45. The Bürgermeister's Wife's Account: Another true tale about discipline, the old use of the rod.

page 46. The Last Queen of France: Her name, Maria Antonia, Archduchess of the Austro-Hungarian Empire, daughter of Empress Maria Theresa, was changed on her marriage to Marie Antoinette.

page 57. The Islanders: I found the Islanders on Turks and Caicos to be an admirably proud and independent people. The third ear in the first section refers to the taxi driver's cell phone. And no, it didn't snow there, but the temperature can turn as raw as cold and emotion.

page 67. Sister Maria Celeste, Galileo's Daughter: Galileo had three children with his housekeeper Marina Gamba. The son, Vincenzio, was eventually legitimized and married into a good family. When Virginia/Sister Maria Celeste was thirteen, for economic reasons, she entered the Convent of San Matteo with her sister Livia.